THE VALE OF FFESTINIOG
AND ITS HINTERLAND

Looking down on Llechwedd slate quarry and Llyn Ffridd y Bwlch

Note:

Some of this material has been published before, in my previous books
Meironydd's Story, Gods and Heroes in North Wales,
Figures in a Landscape and *Gateways to Snowdonia.*

New edition: 2013

ISBN: 978-1-84527-225-1

Cover design: Carreg Gwalch

Published by Gwasg Carreg Gwalch,
12 Iard yr Orsaf, Llanrwst, Wales LL26 0EH
tel: 01492 642031
fax: 01492 641502
email: books@carreg-gwalch.com
website: www.carreg-gwalch.com

Afon Dwyryd up the vale from Maentwrog

Carreg Gwalch Guides

THE VALE OF FFESTINIOG

and its hinterland

A Historical Guide by
MICHAEL SENIOR

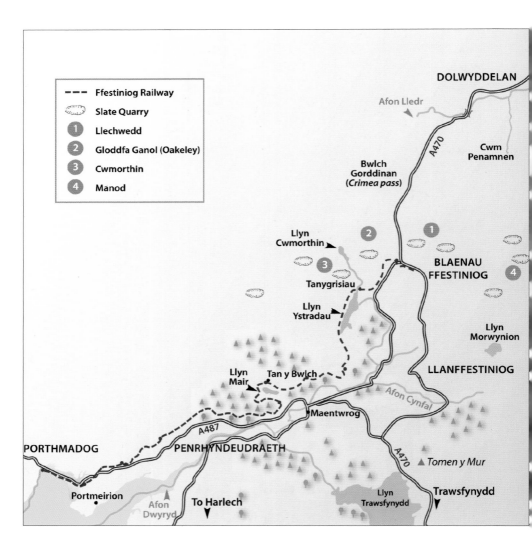

The Vale of Ffestiniog from its estuary to its hinterlands

Contents

The Lledr valley at Pont y Pant

Cwm Penamnen

ONE

The Northern Approach

The valleys have been scoured and softened by their rivers, and two of the rivers which run through this book are formed out of coalescing streams which drain, in opposite directions, the vast folded upland mass lying between Beddgelert and Ysbyty Ifan, some fourteen miles of largely nondescript hillscape. This has not been of much use to anyone over the centuries (though some Bronze Age finds in the Lledr Valley attest to the stubbornness of early adventurers) but its extent and its hill-grasses have provided the ground for large sheep farms; and it is not until the Teigl meets the Cynfal, on the one hand, at Pont Tal-y-bont, and the Lledr on the other hand meets the Diwalaned at Gorddinan farm, that we get any sense of definition.

The valleys, rivers, and so the roads run east to west, and west to east, but right across this unpromising terrain from north to south runs the first long-distance line of communication of historical times, Sarn Helen, the Roman legionary road which linked the Roman fort Canovium in the Conwy Valley with their outpost at Tomen y Mur, south of Ffestiniog. Quite clearly visible for much of its route, it runs as a navigable track from Pentre Du, across the road from the Miners' Bridge in Betws-y-coed, to pitch down steeply in due course into the Lledr Valley at Pont y Pant, from where it follows the river for a short distance and then heads out of the valley again up Cwm Penamnen. Its course up this narrow valley is inevitable, since there is only just room for the road and the river. It may be seen, and indeed used, running as a track along the flat of the valley bottom, and in due course (if I have correctly understood the description of John Cantrell and Arthur Rylance, in their book *Sarn Helen*) doubling back up the slope to emerge from the valley, visible as a diagonal line running upwards from left to right to enter the top of the forest and emerge eventually onto open moorland, in a world where hardly anybody now needs to go.

Sarn Helen is traditionally so named after a Roman empress, Helena, but it must be said that there is more than one candidate for this role. The Mabinogion tale *The Dream of Macsen Wledig* tells us that Helen (here called Elen) was the wife of 'Macsen', a hero based on the historical figure Magnus Maximus, usurping Emperor of Rome: Elen Luyddog, 'Elen of the Hosts', a princess of the ancient British line originating from the pre-Roman king Bran. When she became Empress, still in Britain, she 'thought to have main roads built from each of her forts to the other across the Island of Britain. Because of that they were called the Roads of Elen of the Hosts...' The designation of Roman roads as 'Sarn Helen', Helen's Causeway, is often thought on the other hand to be a reference to the Empress Helena, who became a saint, the mother of Constantine the Great, a generation before Magnus Maximus. However it is also sometimes said to be derived from something quite different: either the description y *leng*, meaning 'of the legions'; or (a more recent speculation), from the Welsh word *elin*, meaning the forearm, perhaps because of the roads' relative straightness.

Elen continues to linger in the area, having, for instance, given her name to a pub, Elen's Castle, and indeed it has been suggested that the name of the town itself should be spelt, in reference to her, with a final 'e'. But 'Dolwyddelan' can be more credibly explained, from the word 'dol' meaning 'meadow', plus the term Irish (*Gwyddel*) in its diminutive form. The little Irishman's meadow.

Although we do not know his name, only his place of origin, the little Irishman is accepted as the founder of the town, and became, under his nickname, the saint to whom the old church is dedicated. 'St Gwyddelan' was most probably one of a small band of Irish missionaries who came to Britain in the 5th and 6th centuries, after the Romans had left, and brought the Celtic version

Elen's connection is kept by a hotel's name in Dolwyddelan

The old church at Dolwyddelan

St Gwyddelan's bell in the church

The Rood Screen in Dolwyddelan's church

of Christianity to a country which had largely lapsed from its Roman Christian conversion.

As it happens St Gwyddelan's church has moved, for reasons which will be dealt with shortly. He originally founded it on the hill which lies between the present church and the castle, Bryn y Bedd, a craggy little hill with a smattering of scrub trees, past which the present main road loops. This is where he had, when he came, raised his cross, an act still remembered in the name of a nearby house, Bod y Groes, the dwelling of the cross. A number of features of the old church moved (we shall see) with the construction of the new one, in about 1500. From the 12th century building which replaced Gwyddelan's presumably simple wooden structure came the Rood Screen, still an impressive feature in the present church. Hanging from its ceiling now is another artefact which long predates the 16th century church: Gwyddelan's bell, a wedge-shaped bell of cast bronze in an old Celtic style, which was dug up in 1850 on the site of the original church and so, quite credibly, is the one brought here from Ireland by the little Irishman himself and rung by him on that hill to call the people of the valley to his services.

In between those two periods Dolwyddelan had decisively been put on the map by the construction of its castle. Traditionally Llywelyn the Great is said to have been born there, but if this is true it is unlikely to have been in the present castle. He was born in the 1170's, and the earliest parts of the building seem to belong to the early decades of the next century. Across the road below the castle, however, is a natural hill, now tree-topped, on which an earlier fortification stood. It is possible that this was the northern Welsh home of Llywelyn's father, Iorwerth. In fact it is likely that the first version of the present castle was built by Llywelyn himself. Its firmly rectangular tower marks it as an early work, before the princes of Wales adopted the new fashion for d-shaped and finally round keeps.

Llywelyn's keep was in fact even simpler than the romantic fortress which we see now; it was only two storeys high, the top section of the present imposing building being a Victorian addition, the work of Lord Willoughby de Eresby. Edward I crucially took Dolwyddelan in the January of 1283, which enabled him to control the Conwy valley and as a result to build his fortress at the crossing at Conwy. At that time he may have raised the castle by another floor, and anyway seems to have made it more spacious; the west tower, which is evidently added, was probably his work. The dressed stone facing of its window, which is also used in the doorway, appears to be Cheshire sandstone, similar to that introduced by Edward at Conwy. At least we can be sure from his accounts for 1283 that work was done at Dolwyddelan immediately after its capture by that Norman king.

The presence of the earlier castle on its knoll provided evidence that the route through this valley was always worth controlling. The fact that the Roman road crossed the valley at right-angles means that a junction of communications took place at an early date. And the motte of an early castle at the side of the Roman road deep in the narrow valley of Penamnen indicates that the Roman route remained in use into Norman times.

Round about the year 1485 the great-grandfather of Sir John Wynne of Gwydir, Maredudd ap Ieuan, moved his family up from Eifionydd to occupy Dolwyddelan castle. At the time it was only partly habitable, but he needed the security of its walls, since the area was then infested with bandits. Maredudd had left Eifionydd because of family feuds, saying he had rather fight with outlaws and thieves than with his own relatives, 'for if I live in my own house in Eifionydd I must either kill my own kinsmen or be killed by them.' Up here in Dolwyddelan however there was then a different problem.

The hospice of St. John at Ysbyty Ifan to the east across the moors, was subject to its own jurisdiction and had, by grant, the right of sanctuary. Over the centuries this had developed into a curious inversion of its intended protection, and it became the haven of outlaws and thieves. "No place within twenty miles about," says Sir John, "was safe from their incursion and robbery."

Dolwyddelan castle

The remains of medieval houses at Penamnen

An artist's impression of Maredudd's house

In due course the castle became too small for Maredudd's expanding family. That would perhaps be surprising were it not for his unusual fecundity. He had ten children by his first wife, two by his second, and three by a third woman. There were also at least six others by less stable relationships. After living in the castle for some years he built himself a large house in Cwm Penamnen, the narrow steep-sided valley south of the town, through which runs the Roman road, Sarn Helen. This runs, as we have just seen, right past the extensive ruins of Maredudd's sprawling house.

When Maredudd moved to Cwm Penamnen, deep in the private world of the cwm, he also moved St Gwyddelan's church. The reason was, Sir John was told by his uncles, that the old church stood in a thicket, where he might too easily be ambushed. The whole of this story is puzzling. It would, first, have been easier to cut down the thicket. Secondly the present church is surrounded by immense and ancient yews, one of which is sometime said to be three thousand years old. This would seem to indicate that the church has always been where it is now located, and perhaps (as many old Welsh churches are) on the site of a heathen religious monument. And yet it seems certain that about 1500 Maredudd had the original church on Bryn y Bedd demolished and this one built.

One reason he might have done this is that from the south-east window you can see the top of Y Garreg Big, and from there you could see his homestead in Cwm Penamnen. Sir John says, in his book *The History of the Gwydir Family*:

> Certain it was that he dared not go to church on a Sunday from his house of Penamnen but that he must have the same guarded with men and have the doors sure barred and bolted and a watchman to stand at Y Garreg Big during divine service (being a rock whence he might see both the church and the house and raise the cry if the house were assaulted).

The church is a charming building with a staunch air of age, a firm beam structure raising its roof with some impressive wooden vaulting at the chancel end. Some materials, probably including the fine old rood screen, came from the older church. 'Gwyddelan's' bell, taking us back to the beginning of Christian worship in the area, hangs in the nave. Of special interest also is the 'Dolwyddelan dragon', a figure carved in low relief on a wooden lintel, depicting a strange snake-like creature with folded wings, a long neck at one end knotted in the middle and a head at both ends, one of which has an extended tongue. Challenged to think up a thing that no-one has ever seen, you could do worse than come up with the Dolwyddelan dragon. The carving came from a demolished church further down the valley, and is thought to represent the Conwy valley water-monster, the 'afanc', which lived in Beaver Pool at Betws-y-coed, from where it caused the familiar Conwy valley floods, until it was dragged by oxen over the hills and deposited in a mountain lake. A mistaken exercise as it turned out: it was not the monster, evidently, which was causing the floods, since they still go on.

The other special feature of the church, and one which alone would justify a visit, is the brass memorial to Maredudd himself. This diminutive portrait shows, in a simple style but with a very high degree of skilled craftsmanship, a man at prayer though in full armour, which we may gather was Maredudd's enforced custom. His eyes are alert, perhaps fixed on the watchman on the rock beyond the south-east window. In ornate Gothic lettering in Latin underneath we are admonished to

> pray for the souls of Meredith ap Ivan ap Robt Esq and Alice his wife who died the 18th day of March 1525 on whose souls God have mercy. Amen.

Dolwyddelan's story has in the years since then been largely uneventful, even seeming now neglected by passing tourism. Some slate quarrying took place in the 19th century but died out as unproductive, compared to its neighbours. A patch of abandoned quarry is all that mars its natural hillsides. The main road from north to south Wales runs through it, but does not pause to admire; it runs faster now because of the improved Crimea Pass,

The 'Dolwyddelan dragon'

Maredudd family memorials in Dolwyddelan church

The road climbing up the 'Crimea' pass from Dolwyddelan

The Blaenau Ffestiniog side of Bwlch Gorddinan

and perhaps the major events in the valley's modern history were the building of this route in the 1850s and its widening and straightening in 2008. Opened in 1854, it took its name from the war which had just broken out at the time in the Crimea Peninsula in Ukraine, on the Black Sea, in which Britain and France set out to stop the Russians expanding into the territories of the decaying Ottoman Empire and thus obstructing valuable trade routes with India. The pass reaches a height of 1,263 feet and is frequently blocked in winter.

The only other way out of the Lledr valley (though it leads to the same upland mass) is the course following the river itself, that taken by the railway, up the valley to the scattered farms of Blaenau Dolwyddelan, an area known as Roman Bridge after its crossing of the infant Lledr and the station on the branch line. The bridge is not of course Roman, but the term is familiar as a way of describing something of undoubted ancient origin, and the mood and aspect of this place is much more ancient than Rome. As you penetrate further towards the river's birth from tributaries draining the harsh slopes of the enclosing massif the winding lane takes you far from the predicaments and values of the present, or indeed anything recent. The smell of hill-grass and the peaceful presence of Welsh Black cattle set up their own sound climate. At the cwm's end there is visibly no way out, and the lane fades out in natural vegetation, indigenous scrub oak, birch, rowan and hazel tapering off into grassland and mountain rock.

The pass, carrying the main road, soars clear of this with, now, visible determination. At its peak it reaches the watershed between the two counties of Conwy and Meirionydd, and more than that, the watershed between two very different worlds.

TWO

Blaenau Ffestiniog

The approach to Blaenau Ffestiniog from the pass has often been compared to the entrance to the underworld, an image it owes to the fact that here the land has been turned upside down. What we see in monstrous dark grey heaps is the raw material of the world, normally covered over by a soft green overlay. It seemed for a long time that since the topsoil has been submerged it would never re-establish itself, but gradually now (as in the coal valleys of south Wales) vegetation is starting to stabilise soil on even these inert slopes. Now rhododendrons, colonising the slopes, for instance above and around the Llechwedd quarry 'village', subdue the harshness of the context. But nothing can relieve the view ahead, as one comes down the pass, of the Oakeley quarries, which shock by their sheer size.

There is no getting round the fact that Blaenau existed from its start as a massive commercial enterprise, and indeed it calls itself proudly now 'the town that roofed the world'. It is impossible not to feel the weight of history looming over it, the past hemming it in and blocking its views, the rising slate-tips of the quarries forming a dark, ominous skyline, crags of bedrock jutting into and hanging over its street.

The discovery of a slate vein here in the 18th century led to the opening of a quarry first at Diffwys, the quarry which looms over the edge of the town and gives its name to the town's main square, then on land owned by the Oakeley family. There a Liverpool slate dealer named Holland set up a quarrying business, and it was when his son Samuel arrived in 1821, then aged eighteen, that the rather haphazard industry became organised into a major progressive force. Only four years later Samuel had the quarries

The Oakeley quarry and Llyn Bwlch y Ffridd from the pass

'Old Ffestiniog' re-created at Llechwedd quarry

An underground experience for visitors at Llechwedd quarry

A slate waste tip

The underground deep train at Llechwedd

of Blaenau Ffestiniog producing 10,000 tons of slate. Of course young Samuel Holland came along exactly at the right time. A pivotal point in social history had been reached with the introduction of steam power. As long as the Industrial Revolution had been based on water power, it tended to perpetuate a scattered population. The introduction of steam-power in the late 1760's changed that. It required large numbers of people to be in the same place, and led to the depopulation of the countryside and the equivalent building of towns. Many of these doubled in size in the first half of the 19th century, and of course all the houses in them also had to be roofed. Blaenau Ffestiniog itself was among them. By the beginning of the next century, in 1901, starting a hundred years earlier as a scattered smattering of farmsteads, it was the second largest town in north Wales by population, with a workforce in place of 4000 people.

Blaenau's slates are unusual in several ways, not least their fine fissile quality and their durability, but one characteristic of the geological form here is that it lies mainly, sometimes completely, underground. Slate is formed by extreme pressure from one side, and normally lies in veins between two bands of hard rock. These deposits were originally horizontal, but through movements beneath the earth's surface have become tilted, so that the work of extracting them quickly becomes subterranean. The best of the slate here at Blaenau Ffestiniog lies deep underground. Hence Blaenau's slate works are mines rather than quarries. The Oakeley quarry already mentioned became the largest underground quarry in the world. Its operation involved the use of fifty miles of railway track.

The Hollands were only one of several families which came into this area in the 19th century and introduced a new spirit of enterprise. John Whitehead Greaves came from Warwickshire, of a Quaker background, and only ended up here initially by mistake. He was on his way to Canada, to emigrate, but found at Caernarfon, in 1830, such evidence of the slate trade that he became interested, and in partnership with a Worcestershire man took out an option to prospect at Llanberis, with some success where previous attempts had failed. His interest moved to Blaenau Ffestiniog, where some instinct told him that a vast mass of slate lay below Llechwedd, which lay between two existing quarries. Although he went into partnership with both Lord Newborough and William Oakeley it was for some time still touch and go. Prospecting can bankrupt a firm if it takes too long to find the result. Just in time, in 1849, he found it.

Llechwedd's story is not always a happy one, and its troubles point to an inbuilt weakness of the quarrying business which eventually contributed to its decline. It was, like heavy industry of the future century, very much a matter of owners versus workforce. Workers flocked to the quarries and mines at Blaenau from the country far around, and their work conditions and living conditions were appalling. They lived in barracks of minimum standard and only went home, walking for miles over the hills, on Sundays. Gradually, becoming aware of the magnitude of the business, they came to understand the power that they possessed. The system operated on a bargaining process, which so far the owners had controlled. The workforce had rebelled at Penrhyn in 1825 but been quickly pacified. When they rose again, better organised, in 1874, the Penrhyn family could foresee a continuing problem. Eventually they felt forced to act decisively: they closed the mine, in 1896, and since this inevitably worked, the starving quarrymen being forced back to labour, they tried the same response in 1900, leading to a three-year lock-out which effectively destroyed the slate industry. Without Penrhyn in operation the national supply of slates could not meet demand, with the result of the commodity becoming overpriced in relation to competing material. A change of taste to roofing tiles suited the new suburbia, slate roofs becoming seen as belonging to an old and squalid urbanisation, which indeed by then they did.

Penrhyn's problems favoured Ffestiniog's enterprise for a time, but the habit of rebellion is infectious. A strike at Llechwedd in 1892 lasted sixteen weeks, during which time some quarrymen

Streets cling to the rock face at
Blaenau Ffestiniog

The ever-present slate tips

Blaenau Ffestiniog

Slate quays may still be seen on Afon Dwyryd

The Ffestiniog Railway station at Blaenau

were forced by the demands of poverty to return to work. The story of the tensions and conflicts is well presented at the preserved quarry 'village' at the present tourist facility at this still operating mine. A train or a lift will take you underground into illuminated caverns to see what, at the time, was only dimly candle-lit.

The Greaves family continued to run Llechwedd, where they had introduced much innovation. J.W. Greaves, who had been there since he first decided to back his hunch in the 1840s, exhibited his slates in the Great Exhibition in 1851, where he won a First Prize medal, and in doing so established the value of Ffestiniog slates. He and his wife retired in 1870 back to Warwickshire, where they lie buried in the parish of Lillington. A daughter of theirs married into the Williams-Ellis family, and hence links up two parts of this valley.

Before J. W. had retired, leaving the running of the business to his sons, he had been much involved with the setting up of the Ffestiniog railway. This had started to carry slates down to the port at Porthmadog in 1836, and although Greaves resented the high tariffs charged by the railway company he eventually decided to join what he could not beat, and became treasurer and eventually Chairman of the company.

To begin with the slates had come down the mountain on the backs of pack ponies, to be loaded in the Vale of Ffestiniog into carts, then shipped from small quays on the river Dwyryd down to its confluence with the Glaslyn, where, on the tidal sands, deep-water vessels were beached which were to take it to its destinations. The pressures of the newly global commerce meant that much of this must change, and a coming-together of technology and new economic habits made this possible.

Quarries had used wagonways since the sixteenth century, and Lord Penrhyn had a five-mile track constructed between 1800 and 1801 to carry his slates from Penrhyn Quarries to Port Penrhyn. It was the development of steam power that was new. The earliest railways were powered by horses and by gravity, the horses which pulled them up riding back down in them with the slate. During the first half of the 19th century steam was the force which drove the Industrial Revolution, and Holland's wagons were first driven by steam engines in October 1863.

Clearly the development of the slate and stone industries benefited greatly from the improved techniques of railways, and railways, on the other hand, owe their origins to the rise of the stone industry. Blaenau Ffestiniog's history sits in the pivot of this symbiosis, since as the slate business eventually declined, in the early twentieth century, the town found itself at the hub of branch lines.

The Ffestiniog narrow-gauged railway had from the start managed to combine business with pleasure, since its recreational potential was evident as soon as it existed, and it started to carry passengers from as early as 1865. Ironically the junction of lines which now gives it added attraction brought about its initial decline. The long tunnel under Bwlch Gorddinan was built by 1879, and two of the major quarries (Llechwedd and Oakeley, on the northern side of the town) started to use the new Conwy Valley line to carry their slates down to the Conwy, to be shipped at the slate quay at Deganwy, rather than to Porthmadog. By the 1920s the Ffestiniog narrow-gauge line had become mainly a tourist attraction, and during the next war it closed to passengers. It closed completely in 1946, and was only re-opened in 1983 after decades of restoration. The line carried passengers again from Porthmadog to Tan y Bwlch in 1958, but for a long time got no further. A new section had to be built to bypass the flooding of the old one by the hydro-electric works at Tanygrisiau.

The decline in the demand for slate arose, as we have seen, from the combination of several factors, ranging from industrial politics to fashion. But it was perhaps inevitable anyway, roofing slate being a product of its time. The great urbanisation which resulted from the Industrial Revolution had largely taken place by the beginning of the 19th century. As ports developed, however, the market became wider, and demand went on increasing into the 1870s. The great fire of Hamburg, a port relatively easily reached

The mouth of the railway tunnel under Bwlch Gorddinan

The original station at Tanygrisiau

Manod slate tips from Blaenau Ffestiniog

Van Dyck's portrait of Charles I on horseback passes under an old railway bridge on the road to Manod quarry.

from Porthmadog, in 1842, led to a sudden hunger for Welsh slates. But it was in the end social as well as economic inbuilt problems which led to the slate industry's decline.

It might be expected that the existence of such large holes in the ground would give rise to other uses, but this has been surprisingly rare. In the aftermath of their commercial heyday one event, of which we only became aware much later, stands out. High above Blaenau Ffestiniog to the east lies the mass of Mynydd Manod, and on its shoulder, still only accessible by mountain track, the Manod Quarries. It is said that Winston Churchill became concerned during the darkest hours of the Second World War for the safety of the nation's art treasures, a premonition which was justified shortly after by the danger done, to the National Gallery among much else, by the Blitz. He decided to have the most important paintings moved, and was advised that a suitable place to store them would be underground, where the conditions could be controlled.

The most suitable safe place which could be recommended was, for some reason, Manod Quarry. It was inside the mountain, entered by a tunnel from a narrow doorway, and sufficiently out of sight to remain secret. A nine-month programme of preparation took place, during which the paintings were already dispersed to temporary safe homes. The entrance had to be extended, due to the vast size of many of the works. Five thousand tons of slate were removed from around the entrance, enlarging it from six foot square to thirteen foot by ten. Five chambers were constructed within the cave, in which the humidity and air temperature were controlled. Railway lorries then brought the paintings in, driving into the mountain. The only problem arose with the height of a railway bridge carrying an old quarry railway (now long disused) over the road, which proved too low for Van Dyck's portrait of Charles I on horseback and Piombo's painting of the raising of Lazarus. The road surface had to be lowered by two and a half feet, and, some accounts add, the vehicle's tyres deflated. The bridge is still exactly the same but now rather ivy-covered, carrying the old line over the start of a long mountain road up to the Manod quarry. That business, still a working quarry also known as Bwlch, lies hidden from Blaenau and everywhere else at the back of the large hump of Manod mountain.

Manod was kept by the Government after the war, half expected to be used again if the Cold War conditions deteriorated. It required court action by the putative owner in the early 1980s to regain use of it, and a programme of untopping has resulted in open-cast use.

When the National Park was drawn up in 1950, Blaenau Ffestiniog was deliberately excluded, and it still bears a ring around it on the map. This was mainly, as would be thought, because it was ugly and industrial, unsuited to National Park status; but also because it was hoped that industry would be attracted to revive it, since with the vanishing of its raison d'etre it had declined into depression, and the restrictions on development which went with National Park status would hamper this. Not much, however, resulted from this hopeful ploy, and now it is seen that encouraging tourism is a more promising option. The population then marooned by the failure of their one-industry economy tended, if they could, to leave. Blaenau had become a place to avoid. It was presumably because of, rather than in spite of, this temporary pariah status, that the town's most famous resident arrived, in May 1955, from the more respectable surroundings of Corwen.

John Cowper Powys had achieved cult status by then as a romantic novelist, and latterly his work had had a Welsh setting. He was born in Derbyshire and spent his childhood in Somerset, where his father was a vicar. This widespread displacement became a feature of his life. He spent much time in America, where he eventually met the woman who became his permanent partner (though they never married), Phyllis Playter. They lived in a small terraced cottage just up from the main road in Blaenau, which now bears a plaque to record this. When Powys died in 1963 Phyllis continued to live there, for another nineteen years, a little old

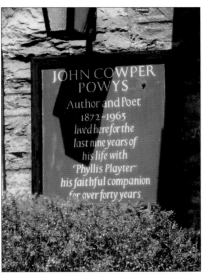

A plaque now marks the cottage which was the home of the novelist John Cowper Powys

David Nash's artowrk

New street art in slate now celebrates Blaenau's history

Llyn Ystradau, Tanygrisiau

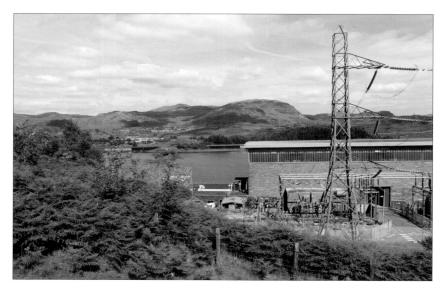

Tanygrisiau hydroelectric powerhouse

American woman in black, in the Greek style of widowhood, who still retained her Kansas accent.

Phyllis had no telephone, so arrangements to meet had to be done by postcard. Nevertheless, having been put in touch by a friend, I used to visit her regularly during the 1970s. It was a cosy, comfortable cottage, with welcoming hospitality. She had adopted the Welsh custom of producing a cake straight from the oven.

In the 1960s some revival took place with the construction of the Tanygrisiau hydro-electric scheme, one of the first major pumped storage enterprises in the United Kingdom, and at the time the largest such plant in the world. It was opened by the Queen in 1963. This innovation in technology, now better exemplified by the vast scheme at Dinorwig, works by the application of reasoning as well as water-power. Electricity is cheaper at certain times, for instance at night, than at others such as in the morning, by the operating of the market force of demand. It therefore shows a profit if cheap electricity can be used to provide expensive electricity, so the pumping up from Tanygrisiau to Stwlan dam takes place at night, the emptying of the lake at Stwlan into the turbines housed below happens in the morning. Ffestiniog's power is also available in an emergency, since it is Britain's fastest generating plant, producing 360 megawatts in one minute. Twenty-seven cubic metres per second fall through shafts leading to concrete tunnels. The power station, consisting mainly of a large turbine hall on the bottom reservoir, Llyn Ystradau, has now retreated from involvement with tourism, presumably as demand dropped off when it no longer seemed like a new enterprise.

Above Tanygrisiau, reached from the parking area by a steep footpath beside a waterfall, is the hidden quarry valley of Cwmorthin. Started in 1810 the quarries here flourished for a time in the 1870s, when about two hundred families lived in this enclosed mountain haven. Originally, as can be seen, gouged into shape by a glacier, before the 19th century it was home already to an old farming community and, it is said, a drovers' route, and the ruins of farmhouses may be found here; but it is from the quarries' working period that the shells of buildings remain which are now the subject of an attempt at preservation. Here there are the remains of a chapel which served the evidently settled population and the terraces of cottages they lived in, together with (rather surprisingly) a manor house, Plas Cwmorthin, once the home of the manager of the quarry, now a ruin among some trees. These remains are all now (in 2013) the subject of appeals and applications to fund their rescue from the danger of collapse.

The quarry here was always problematic, being beset by bad working conditions and lack of safety measures. Known locally as the Slaughterhouse, Cwmorthin had the unfortunate distinction of suffering twenty-two deaths out of a workforce of 550 between the years 1875 and 1886.

The workings were around the lake, Llyn Cwmorthin, and the shafts were at lake level and worked upwards into the mountain. There, in the bowels of Allt Fawr, they met the Oakeley mine-shafts coming the other way. After major collapses in both mines in the 1880s the New Welsh Slate Company, which tried to revive Oakeley, purchased the failed business at Cwmorthin. This did not, however, revive, and attempts at renewal in the 1920s and 30s only kept it going sporadically, and it in effect became part of the Oakeley works, to which it was joined underground. Now it is a favourite pitch for potholers, having miles of tunnels and vast chambers, as well as many abandoned artefacts from its working days.

Cwmorthin's deserted buildings are deteriorating fast, particularly in danger being the last remaining few dwellings of the terrace of (originally) eight (later thirteen) quarrymen's cottages ('Tai Llyn') built in the 1860s, the one tall chimney which is left being not expected to last much longer without help. The Friends of Cwmorthin, who make all this information available to us, are working on raising the money to rescue what remains, and hoping to institute a heritage trail around the site.

Few surprises have arisen in the intervening years to disturb Blaenau's staunch resilience. Blaenau attracts the sort of people

Cwmorthin

Head of the Cwmorthin tramline

Artefacts of slate now greet the visitor approaching from the station

who are, by their nature, rare. The artist David Nash, R.A., though born in Surrey, has been faithful to his adopted home since he moved here in 1967, and has worked in the meantime in a chapel on the Tanygrisiau road close to the northern edge of the town; an example of his work (a giant construction in metal) can be seen by the main road heading back towards the pass.

Now however this attitude of quiet stubbornness has changed, since Blaenau has decided to re-invent itself. Four and a half million pounds have (so far, in 2013) been spent on street art, surfaces, interpretation. The broad scheme is co-ordinated by an umbrella body, Blaenau Ymlaen, which unites the various regenerating groups. The aim has been to tackle the usual problems, the symptom of empty shops and the mutual reinforcement of the lack of work and a dwindling population. The County Council and the Welsh Government contributed, but the bulk of the funding came from the European Union in the form of a grant specifically aimed at regenerating town centres. This meant that the focus of the scheme had to be the main street, which includes the arrival point for visitors coming on the narrow-gauge railway. Here a gateway feature, a magnificent set of slate pillars, rears above the steps which lead the visitor (it is hoped) up from the station and into the town. A viewing platform, under a canopy, with a view of the spread of the Moelwyns, acts as a bus stop and focal point at the top of the steps. Diffwys Square, site of the original station (which is next to be restored) has been embellished with further artefacts of slate, the dense symbolism and layers of imagery of which can best be opened up by acquiring the little booklet which interprets them, and also acts as a guide to the town trail of inscriptions, sayings from Blaenau's industrial past and colloquial present which are set into the pavement. The aim of all this, along with considerable visual improvement of shops, is explicitly to "turn Blaenau Ffestiniog into an important visitor destination" (as the Economy Cabinet Member said), and whether this will work is of course a matter to be decided by time. For the present the scheme has won prestigious awards for its use of public art in an engineering enterprise.

This focus on the town centre, to some extent led by the restrictions of the grant, is compensated for by the activities of Antur Stiniog, a parallel body which was set up to make new use of the damaged countryside nearby. Antur Stiniog is a trail centre, specialising in downhill cycling using quarrymen's tracks, where you can cycle all day without even pedalling. An 'uplift shuttle' takes you back up. There are also plans for a 'velorail', a pedal-powered railway making use of disused railway tracks. This activity, popular in France, is at present unknown in the United Kingdom. In 2014 - zip wire - more details please

Since 2010 a campaign has been carried out to include the town in the Snowdonia National Park, the town council arguing that it would help to encourage visitors to stay and spend in the town. It was reported that the 150,000 people a year who arrive on the Ffestiniog railway were found by a survey to spend an average of 22p each in the town.

Antur Stiniog – offering adventure bikes on well-planned tracks above Llechwedd quarry

Blaenau'r quarry tracks now form cycling tracks

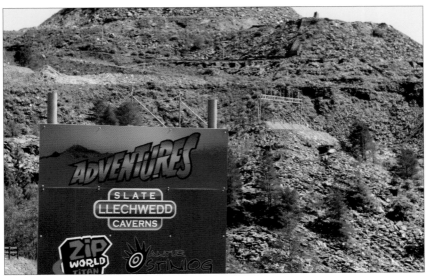

Llechwedd, still a working quarry, gives visitors a full experience of the slate industry and modern adventure attractions

Y Pengwern – today a community co-operative inn

Llanffestiniog church

THREE

The Central Valley

'Blaenau' means literally the tops, the ends, the tips of something, and carries the sense of coming before the thing it refers to: the approaches to Ffestiniog. It is Ffestiniog which is, or was, the main place, the small clustered village with its scattering of outlying cottages and farms which is now called, to distinguish it from its larger neighbour, Llanffestiniog, sometimes shortened to Llan. It centres on a church and a pub. The latter, the Pengwern, perhaps provides the way to understand it, because that was originally called Yr Efail, the Smithy, and it grew its role by being at the start of the long journey over the moors which the drovers used to take, up onto the Migneint on the way to Bala, or to Pentrefoelas, and to England.

They used to gather here to shoe the animals before the moorland crossing. That was mainly in the 18th century, and sometime in the 19th Yr Efail became the Pengwern Arms Hotel. As such, and because of its point at a significant geographical junction, it attracted passing travellers. George Borrow, for instance, stopped here briefly, made a cryptic remark, and moved on. The novelist Elizabeth Gaskell and her husband had visited Ffestiniog on their wedding tour, and later, in 1844, stayed at the inn. It was here that their son William caught scarlet fever, of which he subsequently died. His death led to Mrs. Gaskell's first novel, *Mary Barton*, which she wrote as therapy for her bereavement.

The importance to our landscape and rural history of the droving industry lies in a combination of several factors. From the 17th century onwards the drovers formed a significant branch of social life. For one thing, at the height of their activity, they were extremely numerous. Thousands of head of cattle moved from the breeding grounds of Llŷn and Anglesey via the markets of Shrewsbury and Hereford to the English meadows, where they were fattened to produce the roast beef of Old England. The men who accompanied them played several roles. They were the carriers of money in the form of written bills, the origins of a banking system. They bore letters to relatives in the cities, and most importantly of all they carried news. Llanffestiniog was an important place, for a time, when the droves moved constantly through it.

Then all this came to an end when, in the second half of the 19th century, the railways provided an easier way of moving cattle and pigs from Wales into England. Suddenly Llan, and its pub, lost their traditional use. For a long time they continued to provide a stopping place for travellers, though this was never a major travellers' route. Then in the early months of 2009 the pub closed.

In a way this was the start of a new, and unexpected, life for it. Some local people got together, decided to do something about this situation, and the next year held a public meeting. Pengwern Cymunedol, the Pengwern Community, had come into existence. It formed itself into an "industrial and Provident Society", a community initiative run for the benefit of the village, managed by a Board of Directors elected by the shareholders of the company. Shareholders consisted of anybody who bought £100 of shares, and all shareholders, regardless of how many shares they have, have one vote each. More than £25,000 was raised by this means, and various public grants followed. The pub opened again in May 2011.

One function that Llan Ffestiniog still has is as a point of entry into the Cynfal valley. The river Cynfal rises on the moors and runs energetically down beside the B4391 to fall unexpectedly into a wooded gorge, giving rise to a striking waterfall. It is an essentially hidden place, and we would not attach much significance to this river and valley if it had not, somehow, been chosen as the setting for a quite remarkable story.

The story forms the 'Fourth Branch' of the Mabinogion, *Math*

The head of Cwm Cynfal and Cynfal river

A secluded meadow in Cwm Cynfal

Meadowsweet

Tomen y Mur

Fab Mathonwy, which tells the story, among other episodes, of the love affair of Lleu and Blodeuwedd. Lleu had been cursed by his mother Arianrhod with never having a wife of the human race. In mythology, and particularly in this tale, the apparently impossible somehow without contradiction takes place. His uncle the wizard Gwydion makes for him a woman out of flowers, specifically the flowers of the oak, the meadowsweet, and the broom, indigenous wild flowers common in the Welsh countryside in its flush of early summer. Two of the ingredients were perhaps added to give the figure substance and strength. Exactly what is meant by the flower of the oak is not clear, as it might perhaps be the mistletoe, given its attested importance for the druids. The broom is said by some to bear the smell of female sexuality. It is the meadowsweet, hesitantly dancing in the meadows in the breeze, petalled heads on vulnerable stalks, sweetly scented, each bloom (though many are there) in pretty and individual self-display, which would do on its own as a record of the essence of femininity. Gwydion, with the help of his kinsman Math, succeeded in making the most beautiful woman ever seen.

To celebrate Lleu's marriage to her, Math, king of Gwynedd, gave him an area of his kingdom, the territory now known as Eifionydd and Ardudwy, and Lleu founded his court at Mur Castell, now known as Tomen y Mur. To this place came, while Lleu was away hunting, a passing neighbouring lord, Gronw Bebyr, lord of Penllyn, which is the east side of Bala lake. Gronw fell for Blodeuwedd, there on her own. Who could resist a woman made of flowers?

They plan (like Clytemnestra and Aegisthus) the way to dispose of Lleu on his return. This is not a straightforward matter, since Lleu is of the class of hero who can only be killed under certain unlikely circumstances. Delilah-like Blodeuwedd winkled out of him the details of his fateful secret. The theme is that of being between two worlds, where things are neither this nor that, since he can be killed neither within a house nor outside, neither on horseback nor on foot, and (it appears) neither on water nor dry land. He tells her however how these multiple contraries can be reconciled, and as a result we find him in due course trustingly perched with one foot on the back of a goat and the other on the edge of a bath-tub, under a canopy of thatch on the bank of the river Cynfal near their home.

The story is specific. The lover and conspirator hid himself "under the lee of a hill which is now called Bryn Cyfergyr", a remarkable outcrop called (now) Bryn Cyfergyd, which overlooks the steep valley. From there he throws a spear which kills the near-immortal Lleu, perched in his highly ritualistic tableau on the Cynfal's bank.

His soul flies away as an eagle and his uncle Gwydion eventually tracks the bird down in the Nantlle valley below Snowdon and restores Lleu, by his magic, to human form. The hero and magician then set off together to confront Lleu's wife and her lover. Up at Tomen y Mur Blodeuwedd knows they are coming, and she and her maidens set off from the court in fear, cross the mountain and the Cynfal river in its upper cwm, and flee towards the moorland. Foolishly they all looked back in fear as they went, with the result that the maidens, walking ahead, stumbled backwards into a lake and were drowned. Llyn Morwynion, 'lake of the maidens', still lies up there, a shallow moorland lake with a lip overlooking not only the upper Cynfal but a fine distant view down to Traeth Mawr and the Porthmadog coast, and out beyond the bay to the Llŷn peninsula. To come up over that edge and onto the moorland backwards would be quite demanding, but then to proceed to fall into the lake would require an unusual degree of carelessness. Their mistress, in any case, did not follow her maidens to that end. And there it was, at the edge of that moorland lake, that Gwydion caught Blodeuwedd up.

She was confronted not only by his terrible and rightful anger, but by his magic powers. He turned her there and then into an owl - another reference, in this story so rich in allusion, to the belief in the transmigration of souls. An owl she still is, and you can hear her in the Welsh woods bemoaning her fate. 'Blodeuwedd' is, the

Bryn Cyfergyd may be seen in the distance from the site of Gronw's stone

Gronw's stone, for a long time lost, has now been set upright

The field where the stone is – still called Bedd Gronw, Gronw's grave

Llyn Morwynion

tale says, still 'owl' in our language, and it may once have been, meaning as it does 'flower-face'.

The lover, meanwhile, all too aware of his likely fate, retreated towards Bala, and sent messages to Lleu offering compensation. These were haughtily refused, and instead Lleu demanded that he undergo the same trial as he himself had done, standing as target on the banks of the Cynfal. As it seems every man has done since Adam, he blamed the woman for having set him up. Persuaded by this Lleu relented, and allowed him the chance of holding up a slab of slate between his body and the spear-blow. But there was no avoiding fate. The spear went straight through it, and through him. "And there the stone is, on the bank of Cynfal river in Ardudwy, and the hole through it".

At some point, then, before the tale took its final written form in the late 14th century, there clearly was such a stone in this river valley. It may have been the cause of the tale, or the tale's detail; or it may have been provided because the tale demanded it. Some work could be done on this, but at present we do not know which way the cause-to-effect route went. In any case it then seems that the stone in question disappeared, and when I researched *Portrait of North Wales* I concluded it was no longer there. Lady Charlotte Guest made no mention of it in her otherwise comprehensive notes to her edition of the Mabinogion, in 1848. A writer called Frank Ward wrote in 1935 that it had been said in 1830 that a stone answering the description had stood on the banks of the Cynfal within living memory. After extensive search he himself found a slab with a hole in it, at the time filled with moss, but since it measured only forty to forty-two inches in height it does not form an adequate representative of Gronw's stone, and in any case that stone has not been found again since. The search remained unsuccessful, until one day in the early weeks of 1990.

A local teacher and historian, Geraint Vaughan Jones, had been looking for the stone for some time, but was on the hillside above the Cynfal with a friend attempting to trace the route of Sarn Helen in its passage across the Cynfal valley. Quite by accident they found what appears to be the stone referred to, half buried, the hole in it covered with moss but still visible. It lay not on the bank of the Cynfal but alongside a small tributary, known as Afon Bryn Saeth, from the name of the farmhouse nearby, Bryn Saeth. Like other place names in the area this too is a reference to the story: the hill of the arrow, being supposedly the place where Lleu made the spear which killed Gronw.

The stone disappeared again for a time, but I had been told where it was and found it lying on the ground and covered with leaves.

It is a smooth, nearly rectangular but slightly tapered slab, some five foot six inches in length from toe to head, with a hole about four and a half inches in diameter approximately five inches from the head. It has been set upright now in the wooded corner of the field known as Bedd Gronw, Gronw's grave, and is sited undoubtedly on a riverbank above and within view of the Cynfal itself. It is unmarked and inconspicuous now, as if, like the Holy Grail, you can only find it by chance. This clearly deliberate attitude of inconspicuousness is in keeping with the old stone's mystery and, over the ages, reclusiveness.

Lleu and Blodeuwedd, and subsequently Gronw, lived not here but nearby, up at the site of the Roman camp at Tomen y Mur, known in the tale as Mur Castell. The site is perhaps most notable now for its view of a nuclear power station, now closed (since 1991) and in the long process of being decommissioned. Up at Tomen y Mur (on private land, requiring permission from the farmer to view them) are the ruins of Roman baths and the outline of something thought to have been a small amphitheatre. Nearby is a large mound on the exposed hillside, said to be the motte of a medieval castle, looking much like a large burial mound. The location of all these features here is explained by the Roman road system, since the great trunk route called Sarn Helen crossed the moor here and at this point met the link road coming up from the legionary fort of Segontium, modern Caernarfon.

Figures in myth become associated with ancient sites, and it is perhaps the pillar close by the outside wall of the church at

Cwm Cynfal

Tomen y Mur

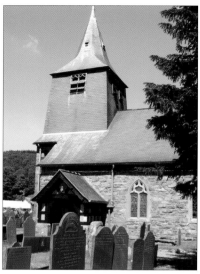

Twrog's stone against the wall of the church, giving Maentwrog its name

The Oakeley Arms at Maentwrog

Maentwrog, after which the church and village are named, 'Twrog's Stone', which ties another great Mabinogion hero, Pryderi, king of South Wales, to this area. For reasons which unfortunately cannot concern us here he finds himself confronted with the northern Welsh magician Gwydion, the uncle of the hero of the Cynfal story, in hand-to-hand combat on the sands of Traeth Mawr. The two stood in front of their armies on that great stretch of estuarial marsh, now reclaimed and tamed, which formed the silt-plain of the river Glaslyn as it drained the Snowdon range into Tremadog Bay. Pryderi, the story tells us, was killed by Gwydion there, 'and at Maen Tyriawg, above Y Felenrhyd, was he buried and his grave is there'. The stone has for a long time been associated with Twrog the founding saint, and is said to have been thrown by him to its present position in order to crush a pagan altar. Most probably the stone itself marks a pre-Christian burial site, the church being set up (as so often) to replace it with a new religion.

The yew trees in the churchyard are thought to be more than a thousand years old, but the church itself as it is now is comparatively modern, having been rebuilt in 1814, and restored by the Oakeley family in 1896. That Maentwrog village also has a sound consistency about it is also due to its being on the great Oakeley estate.

FOUR

The Lower Valley

One of the initial puzzles of this area is the question of what happened to the Oakeleys. The family went from almost unimaginable wealth to ruin in an example of hubris dramatically contained within the bounds of the 19th century. After a brief period of quarrying at the start of that century they let the rights on their land at what became Blaenau Ffestiniog to those who would develop the industry, notably Samuel Holland (a slate merchant from Liverpool) and his son, also Samuel, then aged eighteen, as we heard in an earlier chapter. William Griffith Oakeley, who inherited in 1811, benefited by a rent-plus-royalty agreement which became prolific as the mines expanded. He set in place what became the family custom of spending vast sums of money on their lands and buildings.

Most conspicuous among these is the house itself, Plas Tan y Bwlch, now a training and conference centre of the Snowdonia National Park, across the valley from Maentwrog. Set on a grandly landscaped hill, it exudes a pleasant, confident late-19th century splendour: fine wooden panelling within a robust stone-built pile. The portraits of the family, some photographic, attest their heyday. You can sense the awe of the artist or photographer in the presence of such impressive hats and such good tweed.

Plas Tan y Bwlch itself is not mentioned as a house until 1756, by which time it was probably an enlarged version of an earlier dwelling. The Tan y Bwlch estate itself had its origins in the 13th century, and the main part of its vast expansion occurred with the marriage of an owner of it, Robert Evans, to Lowry Price, heiress to property at Gellilydan (south-east of Maentwrog) and to land at Rhiwbryfdir near Blaenau Ffestiniog, that area where the

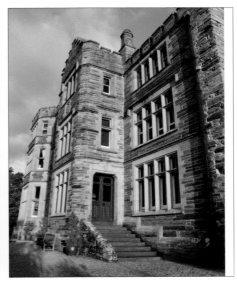

Plas Tan y Bwlch

William Edward Oakeley, the owner of Tan y Bwlch estate 1879-1912

*Oakeley family and friends standing near the terrace steps
at Plas Tan y Bwlch, 1890-1900*

*Some of the Tan y Bwlch Estate staff in a 1905 Daimler outside the east
entrance of the Plas*

mountain turned out to be made of slate, which subsequently became a huge hole in the earth known as the Oakeley Quarry. The Oakeley family themselves did not become involved in this story until 1789, when the sole heiress to the lands here married outside the area, and out of the long convention of increasing the family holdings by marriage to local landowning families, by marrying an Englishman, William Oakeley, son of a Staffordshire clergyman and from an old Shropshire family.

Plas Tan y Bwlch by then had a reputation for good living, which is attested to by Thomas Pennant, whose *Tours in Wales* dates from 1773. Pennant stayed at evidently a predecessor of the Oakeley Arms, which he calls "a very neat small inn", and he says:

> Above it is a house, embosomed in woods, most charmingly situated on the side of the hill. This seat, from the quick succession of owners by the fatal attachment to the bottle, has occasioned many a moral reflection from the *English* traveller.

The leases which William Griffith had so effectively organised eventually expired, and the Oakeley of the time (William Edward, who inherited in 1879) tried to let them again at an exorbitant rate. Only one tenant renewed, and the cost-cutting involved resulted in rock and roof falls in the mines, culminating in the Great Fall of 1882-3, when six million tons of rock fell into the cavern, and among other things hampered extraction for some time to come. William Edward formed the Oakeley Slate Company to run the business himself, but the Oakeleys, ironically, had no direct experience of slate quarrying and proved incompetent at it. It was bad luck on William Edward also that in the years 1883-4 there was a slump in the slate trade. Huge loans were necessary to keep the business going, and the family now found itself in large debt.

This was not helped by the lifestyle of William's son, Edward de Clifford, whose interest in horse-racing got him further into debt. His father had continued to spend lavishly on his Welsh estate, building a school at Maentwrog and extending and renovating the church, formerly St.Mary's, which then became dedicated to St. Twrog. For much of this time the Oakeleys lived in London and elsewhere, adopting the fashionable social life of the period, the end of the 19th and start of the 20th century.

Their creditors however demanded repayment, and most of the Tan y Bwlch estate was put up for sale in 1910 – but almost all of it failed to sell. Edward de Clifford ('uncle Teddy') sold the Tan y Bwlch lands to his niece, Margaret Inge, in 1915, for £25,000, and the family line effectively petered out in the 1950s. The estate ended in the hands of distant relatives, and was sold on the death of the last surviving Oakeley, Mary, who had married William Inge, a landowner of the Tamworth area; she had inherited the property at Tan y Bwlch from her daughter Hilda who died unmarried in 1953. Mrs Inge died in 1961, aged ninety-six. The residue of the estate, including the house, was then sold for the first time, in 1962. After some unsuccessful attempts to find uses for it the Plas itself was acquired by the two County Councils administering the National Park, and the Countryside Commission, in an inspired resolution, to form the Study Centre of Snowdonia National Park, opening as such in 1975.

Much of the effect of the Oakeley spending still survives, in, for instance, the thirteen acres of Victorian landscape in which the house is set. Down the hill from the Plas is the substantial inn in the same building style, the Oakeley Arms, and a little above the family seat is the beautifully serene private lake, Llyn Mair. This artifical fourteen acre lake was constructed by William Edward to form a 21st birhday present for his daughter Mary, or Mair, but it also served a practical pupose. A pipeline ran from its foot to a power house behind the house, and enabled Plas Tan y Bwlch to be self-supplying in electricity, which thanks to a successor hydro-electirc scheme it still is. The road uphill from the Oakeley Arms runs alongside this lake, flanked on its upper side by natural primal woodland banked over the peaceful lake, before pitching down through Rhyd to Garreg, where it meets the A487.

Where the latter road comes down from Aberglaslyn, following the edge of the silt plain of the Glaslyn river (long ago reclaimed as

William Edward Oakley and his wife, Mary, on horseback, 1890s

Llyn Mair

Cnicht above Cwm Croesor

Plas Bron Danw

In Bron Danw gardens

farmland) a lane branches sharply up to Cwm Croesor, traditionally the home of writers and artists because all very much part of the world presided over, owned, and to a large extent invented, by Clough Williams-Ellis. At the start of this the house where he lived dominates its little valley, Plas Brondanw, the ancient family home of half of his surname, the Williams family. The hyphenated name is in fact a clue to his inheritance, since when the Williamses of Plas Brondanw married the Ellises of Glasfryn, on the Llŷn peninsula, a vast amount of land came into their joint possession, most of it still owned and occupied now by branches of the family. The amalgamated family favoured their property on the Llŷn, and neglected the Croesor territory. Thus it was that when Clough's father gave him the Brondanw estate in 1908 he had a free hand to transform an area of more than 3000 acres, including fifty-three houses and five farms. This went along with the quarrying interests owned by his mother's family, the Greaveses, owners of Llechwedd quarry and of property stretching down to Tremadog. When Clough came into possession of the first part of this, falling from Croesor to Llanfrothen, he was twenty-five. Shortly after he set about acquiring more lands, bringing in the beautiful mountain extents of Cnicht and the Moelwyns.

You cannot move in the Brondanw area without being aware of Clough's influence. It spills out over the surroundings in the form of stone ornaments and ornamental buildings. Much of the surrounding landscape and the style of development remind us that he achieved what he did not just because he wanted to but because he could, having behind his confident stance an enviable talent for decoration and display. The house itself, Plas Brondanw, formed a Welsh base for Clough and, when he married in 1915, his wife Amabel, née Strachey. When they first came there it was divided and let, but as the tenancies expired they took on more and more of it until they occupied the whole.

Plas Brondanw itself originates in the 16th and mid-17th century, and its unrestored state provided Clough with an opportunity for expression, as did also, in a more obvious way, the gardens. These may be enjoyed by the public now, and they notably give views out into the landscape, often carefully framed, as is, for instance, one distant view of Cnicht.

Clough, through his personality, attracted exceptional people, and when he came to settle permanently in Wales (after a long period of being mainly in London) he surrounded himself, whether intentionally or accidentally, with people of distinction in art, literature or academia. Thus, for instance, Patrick O'Brian, the author of a popular series of nautical novels starting with *Master and Commander* in 1969, lived in Croesor with his wife between 1945 and 1949; Jeremy Brooks, best known for his novels *Jampot Smith* and *Smith, as Hero*, but also a major influence in the theatre in the 1960s, acquired a run-down cottage on Clough's estate in Llanfrothen in the 1950s, and died there in 1994; Bertrand Russell lived for the last part of his long life in a fine house on a hill, with a magnificent view, up a private drive between Penrhyndeudraeth and Portmeirion, from which he sent the famous telegrams to Kruschev and Kennedy which many felt at the time had assisted in averting the Cuban missile crisis; he died there in 1970; Michael Burn, known as Micky, distinguished for playing a major part in the Second World War in the apparently suicidal raid on the German U-boat station at St. Nazaire in the Loire estuary, in March 1942, lived nearby. As captain of a troop of commandos he led the assault on the U-boat bunkers under fire, and although he improbably survived was eventually taken prisoner by the Germans and spent some time in Colditz. Burn was not just a war hero, holder of the Military Cross, but a gifted writer (author of some fifteen books) and a war correspondent of The Times. In his youth he managed to have affairs with both Alice Keppel, once the mistress of Edward VII, and Guy Burgess, the communist spy. Such versatility is perhaps characteristic of his wide range of activities in north Wales, and he was throughout his life what might be best described as well-connected. He and his wife were neighbours of the Russells and became close friends with them. I knew him in the 1960s and remember a middle-aged man with a

Portmeirion's waterside setting is a major factor in its atmosphere

Clough's collection of interesting buildings makes Portmeirion hard to define

pleasant round open face and an educated manner. He died aged 97 at his home in Minffordd, Penrhyndeudraeth, in 2010.

Although Clough had, as his background from a young age, this substantial tract of land, the place for which he is best known came to him later, when he bought from his uncle an area of overgrown landscape, formerly an old settlement called Aber Ia. Clough had been looking for a site to found an ideal village, and for some time had considered an island as being most suitable. It did not at first occur to him that with Aber Ia he had found what he wanted, and he thought of it at first as a port for yachting, it being the nearest bit of coastline to his house. When he cleared the jungle and opened up the old house it must have become obvious.

Clough bought what was to become Portmeirion in 1926. He first converted the old house by the sea to a hotel, and then over the next thirty or so years he collected rare buildings from various parts of the country, which he had dismantled, transported and re-erected at Portmeiron. The last item to be added was the Colonnade, a structure formerly in Bristol, added in 1959. Portmeirion has had its times of fame and fashion, most recently when it became nationally known as the location of the television series 'The Prisoner'. In pre-war years it was a favourite retreat of the Duke of Windsor, and Noel Coward wrote his play 'Blithe Spirit' up in the Watch House there during a single week during the war. By the 1970s it received a hundred thousand visitors a year. It was, and remains, a highly personal statement, being explicitly for its creator's personal satisfaction. Heretical, unorthodox, deliberately irresponsible, people said. A folly, an example of architectural levity. The important thing to remember, I think, is that Clough regarded the business of having fun as being a worthwhile and wholly respectable enterprise. "It is serious," I wrote of Portmeirion in *Portrait of North Wales*, "to the extent that all good jokes are serious."

Clough had added his late uncle's house, Castell Deudraeth, to the holding in 1931, intending it to become a hotel as adjunct to the Portmeirion complex, but other pressures got in the way and this was not properly fulfilled until it was reopened, after restoration, in 2001. An early Victorian edifice built by the Liberal MP David Williams, who won the seat of Merioneth in 1868, it lacks all Portmeirion's lightness of spirit. Perhaps it is simply too far from the water. Perhaps what is magic about Portmeirion is its estuarial setting, particularly at night, the incoming tide washing up around it the liquid sounds of the water-birds at the edge of the sea and the Dwyryd.

Above the estuary

Castell Deudraeth

The hotel at Portmeirion

A train leaving Porthmadog station to cross the Cob

The head of the Ffestiniog Railway line at Porthmadog

FIVE

To the end of the line

We have seen through much of this book that a constant sub-theme underlies the lovely natural scenery of the Vale of Ffestiniog: that is, the business of transporting as well as producing slate. To summarise:

In early days the slates came down on pack ponies and mules to the quays on the Dwyryd and then by river boats, some forty of them, to the river mouth at the sandbanks of Traeth Mawr, to be loaded onto exporting vessels which came in at full tide (for years before the embankment was built) and beached there when the tide went out. Carts and sledges replaced pack animals as the bulk of produce grew, and shortly the downhill work gave rise to tramways. It was a quick step from there to the devising of a scheme for a continuous line linking quarry and seaport, at first to be gravity fed and pulled uphill by horses.

A lot of people were against the idea. The boat operators of course campaigned against it. The quarry-owners, such as the Greaves family, resented the proposal that they were to be charged what they took to be an extortionate amount for moving their slates; and it was only when the railway enterprise became inevitable that Greaves joined it and in the end more or less ran it. The Oakeley family was mainly concerned to make sure that they had adequate revenue and privileges from the scheme, and it was, in the end, an Oakeley who initiated the line by laying the first stone, in February 1833. An Act of Parliament had set the project firmly in motion, in May 1832.

The new line opened in April 1836. The coordinated power of gravity and horses gave way eventually, in 1863, to steam, responding to increased demand, by which time 100,000 tons of slate a year were being moved down the line. Passengers soon joined this cargo, a quarter of a million in the first year. Many of these to begin with were commuting to work in the quarries from their outlying villages and farmsteads, enabling a labour-intensive industry to expand at Blaenau. When the slate trade eventually declined they were replaced by tourists.

Much of the line has not altered since its construction, still running through hand-cut tunnels and cuttings now, across magnificent stone ramparts and under soaring stone retaining walls. But not far from the start, coming down from Blaenau Ffestiniog, it is radically different. The 'deviation' was the solution to a problem which arose with the decision to reopen the long-closed line, since a large slice of the area around Tanygrisiau was by then under a lake.

This lake, Llyn Ystradau, was of course the lower half of the pump-storage system already referred to, which had come into being in the 1960s. By then the railway had been closed for some time, and it was evidently not envisaged, in the scheme, that it would one day be reopened. The resurrection of it however started in 1954 and proceeded from Porthmadog step by step upwards (to Boston Lodge the first year, Minffordd the second, Penrhyn the third) to reach Tan y Bwlch in 1958. The ideal of completion of the route was then confronted with the need to undertake a considerable engineering exercise, a two-and-a-half mile deviation involving a 310 yard tunnel. All this was eventually achieved largely by the use of voluntary labour. The station at Tanygrisiau is new, in local terms, being opened in 1978, and the Moelwyn tunnel, below it, alongside the former tunnel which ran through the southern end of what is now the lake, was built by Cornish tin miners, with a local workforce, and opened in 1977. Between these points the new line of the railway hugs the lakeside, and the railway and pump-storage system are intertwined, the track crossing the pipes to the turbines just behind the power station.

Below the lake and the Moelwyn tunnel, at Dduallt, an extraordinary spiral loop takes place, the line of the railway

Two different railway gauges meet at Blaenau Ffestiniog station

The entrance to Tanygrisiau tunnel

The original station at Tan y Bwlch

The line finally approaches Porthmadog along the causeway

74

running underneath itself, to give a required gain in height on the upward run. Here the 'deviation' began in the 1960s, the first sod being cut (where a stone now commemorates the fact) on 2nd January that year.

The station below Dduallt is called Campbell's Platform, having been added for the personal use of Colonel Campbell, who lived in the largely 15th century house visible below the railway, Dduallt Manor. Among other things he was a blasting engineer, and contributed in this role to the construction of the 'deviation' through the 60s and 70s. The next station down, Tan y Bwlch, is where the original railway really began, the first stone being laid here by W. G. Oakeley (as mentioned) in February 1833. The line then does a long but tight loop around the lake, Llyn Mair, through the woods, which ends near Plas Tan y Bwlch, site of a request stop added to serve the National Park study centre at the Plas when the railway was reopened in the 1960s.

One of the spectacular pieces of construction takes place a little further down, the Cei Mawr embankment at Rhiw Coch, where the line runs perched on a sixty-two foot high wall, above the stream bed. Then, as the Vale grows gentler and dramatic interludes diminish, there comes a long and fairly straight run parallel with the road, through tamer country, past 'Penrhyn' (the station for Penrhyndeudraeth), past 'Minffordd', the stop for Portmeirion and the junction with the Cambrian Coast Line, finally to reach the waterfront at Boston Lodge. This (called Boston after Madocks's Lincolnshire constituency) was the focal point of the enterprise of construction of the Cob, the great embankment which confronts the trains and motor vehicles at this point, built between the years 1808 and 1811 to prevent the reflooding of the drained land of Traeth Mawr, the silt-plain of the Glaslyn estuary. The Lodge itself was then the engineer's office and a hostel for the workforce; now the complex at Boston Lodge (Boston Lodge Engineering) is not just still the repair workshop for the Ffestiniog line but a supplier to other enterprises of parts for specialised industrial machinery and rolling-stock.

This was the way into Porthmadog for all traffic from this direction until recently, indeed the way into northern Wales for much of the travel from the south. A modern bypass now provides access to the town from the north, running from a point between Minffordd and Penrhyndeudraeth, along the line of the Cambrian Coast Railway, bypassing also Tremadog and continuing the former road system still as the A487, the Caernarfon road. Work on this started in January 2010 and, completed within budget and seven weeks early at the cost of 35 million euros, it opened in October 2011. Five and a third kilometers long, it involved a bridge across the river and another to take the Ffestiniog Railway over the new road.

The cob came into existence as a result of the decision by Madocks to drain and reclaim the Traeth, and this decision in turn took place partly as the result of a mistake. It was widely thought at the time that the chosen official port for Ireland would be Porth Dinllaen, now a tiny hamlet on the Llŷn peninsula. There was some good reason to suppose this, since it was in some ways more favoured, nautically, than Holyhead. In the first six months of the year 1804 alone 656 vessels set out from there to Ireland. It followed that the road from London to Dublin in the future would take the Shrewsbury rather than the Chester line, thus avoiding the problems of crossing the Conwy and the Menai Strait. Entrepreneurs began to prepare for this, building hotels along the way. The only obstacle to this exercise was the crossing of Traeth Mawr, a tidal marsh. Madocks set out to solve this problem by making it dry land.

Porthmadog itself then came into existence as the result of a further unrelated mistake. In the process of building the cob it was necessary to divert the Glaslyn along it, making it run out through new sluice gates at the western end. An unforeseen result of this was that it gouged a deep pool at the point at which it met the sea. Resourceful as ever, Madocks decided to put this new element to use.

It happened also that at that time there was a need for a

Porthmadog's past is maritime, and this character is evident today

Porthmadog was a major ship-building area as well as a port

harbour. The decision to build one coincided with the arrival in Blaenau Ffestiniog of the younger Samuel Holland, and also with the new technology of steam power. The Act of Parliament instituting the new harbour was passed in 1821, and by the early thirties, as we have seen, there was a direct narrow-gauge railway running to it down from Holland's quarries.

Porthmadog was an established port almost at once, and so before the railway came. Ship-building started there straight away, in 1824, with the launch of the sloop Two Brothers, the first of more than two hundred ships to be built at Porthmadog. These had at once developed into a unique style, known as Western Ocean Yachts, three-masted vessels with slanted bows, fore-and-aft rather than square-rigged (which allowed them to beat to windward with short tacks off a lee shore); they were specifically designed to cope with the sudden build-up of short, high waves off the south-Caernarfonshire coast, with its strong landward drift of tidal current which made progress hard and hazardous for squatter vessels.

By 1873 Porthmadog was exporting 116,567 tons of slate in a year. From then until the end of the century both the slate trade and the ship-building business slowly declined, with a revival in the 1880s and early 90s. The start of the Great War drew a line under this period, since much of Porthmadog's trade had been with Germany. In the meantime the town had expanded at high speed, the population rising from 885 in 1821, when Holland first came, to over three thousand in 1861. Everywhere such sudden expansion has led to problems, and epidemics arising out of slum conditions became serious here in the 1850s.

Coastal trade went on, but the coming of the Cambrian Railway in 1867 removed much of this, slate now going (for the purpose of constructing cities in other parts of Britain) by rail instead of sea. Railways, as it turned out, were to form a large element in Porthmadog's future. The revival of the Welsh Highland Railway (its restoration completed in 2011) has given another dimension to the town's role as a transport hub.

Its seagoing business is now largely only a memory. The boat-building area, Pencei, is now no more than a pub, a seating area, and a car park – once a hubbub of ship-building and servicing, slate loading and trading. Only the sturdy architecture of the old buildings there reminds us of the connection with the Oakeley quarries. Recreation has taken over. A yacht harbour now occupies part of the basin, where once such vast quantities of slate set sail. But while the seafaring has gone, as the main activity of the town, the role of railway-hub is thriving and (now the Welsh Highland Railway is fully operational) seems likely to increase.

Porthmadog now is not essentially a seaside town. The beach is at Morfa Bychan, in the form of Black Rock Sands. There is something of a clear division now between the town and the harbour. Porthmadog the town is rightly proud of its shops, which run unbroken for several hundred yards along its High Street, cheerful and exuberant in the summer, with pavement displays and visual variety, awnings and open doors. In winter it has to be said that this is a grim scene, a reminder of the optimism of investing in a frail and seasonal market. Porthmadog's present generally successful character is a symptom of the resilience and adaptability to change which such fundamentally accidental places cultivate within themselves.

Bibliography

BOLLARD, John K. *The Mabinogion*, Gomer Press. 2006.

BORROW, George. *Wild Wales*, Oxford University Press, 1920.

CATTRELL, John, and RYLANCE, Arthur. *Sarn Helen*, Cicerone Press, 1992.

GODWIN, Fay, and TOULSON, Shirley. *The Drovers' Roads of Wales*, Wildwood House, London, 1977.

HUGHES, Gwyndaf. *House on a Hill*, Snowdonia National Park Study Centre, 1989.

PENNANT, Thomas. *Tours in Wales*, Caernarvon, 1883.

SENIOR, Michael. *Portrait of North Wales*, Robert Hale, 1973.
    Gods and Heroes in North Wales, Gwasg Carreg Gwalch, 1993.
    Meironydd's Story,   "   "   "   1997.
    Figures in a Landscape,   "   "   "   2000.
    Gateways to Snowdonia   "   "   "   2012.

WYNN, Sir John. *The History of the Gwydir Family*, Gomer Press, 1990.

Acknowledgement

The author would like to thank Pryderi ap Rhisiart for insight into the new work at Blaenau Ffestiniog.